W9-BUM-664

PARASITES

Ticks

Kris Hirschmann

KIDHAVEN PRESS™

THOMSON

™

GALE

San Diego • Detroit • New York • San Francisco • Cleveland
New Haven, Conn. • Waterville, Maine • London • Munich

LIBRARY OF CONGRESS CATALOGING-IN-PUBLICATION DATA

Hirschmann, Kris, 1967–
    Ticks / by Kris Hirschmann.
        v. cm. — (Parasites)
    Includes bibliographical references and index.
    Contents: Tiny bloodsuckers—The tick attacks—Hurting the host—Controlling ticks.
        ISBN 0-7377-1782-3 (hardback : alk. paper)
        1. Ticks—Juvenile literature. 2. Ticks as carriers of disease—Juvenile literature.
    [1. Ticks.] I. Title. II. Series.
        RA641.T5H54 2004
        614.4'33—dc21

                                                                    2003010729

Printed in China

CONTENTS

CHAPTER 1

Tiny Bloodsuckers

Ticks are **parasites**, which means they live on and feed from other animals. The animals parasites live on are called **hosts**. Ticks survive by drinking the blood of their hosts.

Tick Basics

Ticks are members of the arachnid family, which also includes spiders, mites, and scorpions. There are about 850 species of ticks. Some of these species are tiny—about the size of the period at the end of this sentence. Others are much larger, measuring nearly an inch in length. Most ticks fall toward the smaller end of this range.

Ticks are divided into two categories: hard and soft. Hard ticks have solid plates covering their backs, and their heads stick out from their bodies. Soft ticks have soft coverings, and their heads are hidden beneath their bodies. Ticks of both types must drink the blood of rodents, dogs, deer, birds, and other creatures—including humans—to live and grow.

Born to Drink Blood

Ticks have several built-in tools that help them get the blood they need to survive. The tick's main blood-drinking tool is its long mouthpart, which is called the **hypostome**. The hypostome is hollow and ends in a sharp point. Its shaft is lined with backward-pointing barbs. These barbs bury themselves in the host's flesh when the hypostome is pulled backward. This

Ticks are parasites that drink the blood of animals and humans.

The tick's pointed hypostome is covered with backward-pointing barbs that dig into the host's skin while the tick feeds.

makes the mouthpart very hard to remove once it has been inserted.

Eight long, jointed legs also help ticks to stay put. These legs grab the host's hair or flesh and cling tight. Once a tick gets a firm hold on its victim, it will not let go until it completes its meal of blood.

A feeding tick needs to drink as much blood as it possibly can. For this purpose nature has given the tick a special expandable body. A tick's **abdomen** grows and grows as the tick sucks blood. After a while the parasite has expanded so much that it looks like a tiny inflated balloon. Some types of ticks have such stretchy abdomens that they can drink up to six hundred times their unfed body weight in blood.

The tick's expandable body swells like a balloon as it fills with blood.

The Tick Life Cycle

Ticks have three main life stages. These parasites begin their lives as tiny, wormlike **larvae**. After a tick larva takes a blood meal, its body changes. It becomes a **nymph**. The nymph, too, must take a blood meal. After the nymph drinks, its body changes into an adult shape.

Female ticks (below, white) lay eggs (right) that hatch into larvae (below right).

eggs will eventually hatch into larvae, which must find new hosts and start the life cycle all over again.

Some types of ticks spend their entire lives on a single host animal. Others drop off after each blood meal, then find a new host when the time comes to drink again. Either way, ticks have no trouble finding the food they need to survive. They are perfectly suited to their bloodsucking lifestyle.

CHAPTER 2

The Tick Attacks

A hungry tick has just one thing on its mind: blood. It goes looking for a host. Nothing will stop or distract the parasite. It will search every single day until it either finds a meal or starves.

Finding a Host

Most ticks find hosts by a process known as **questing**. A questing tick climbs up a long blade of grass or another plant. It might also dangle from a low-hanging tree branch. The tick waves its front legs and waits for an animal to pass by.

Ticks use their sharp senses to figure out when a possible host is near. These parasites can sense carbon dioxide gas, which is produced when animals breathe out. They can also sense heat, movement, odors, and even the shadows of passing creatures. When a questing tick senses any of these things, it extends its front legs even farther and gets ready to grab. The tick will seize any fur or flesh that brushes against its legs.

A questing tick (below) extends its front legs (right) before grabbing onto a host.

Some types of soft ticks do not quest. Instead, they live in the nests or dens of their host animals. They simply hop onto the host's body and grab a quick meal whenever they are hungry. Ticks that follow this lifestyle take frequent small drinks of blood instead of occasional large ones.

Mealtime

After a tick gets onto a host, it wanders around for a while. When it finds a spot it likes, it plunges its sharp hypostome into the skin. It holds tight with its eight

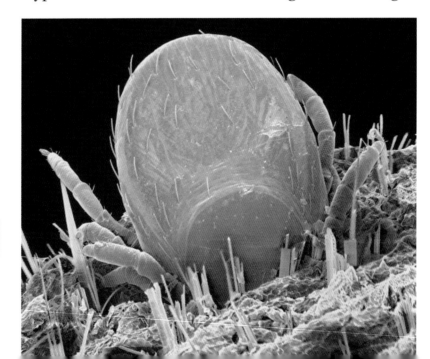

A hungry tick buries its head in its human host.

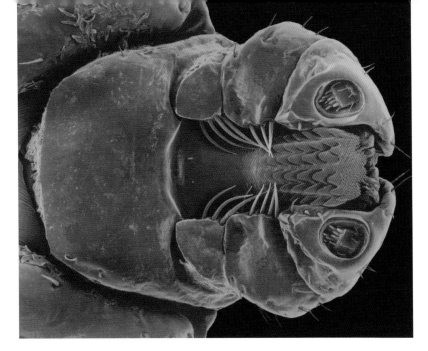

The tick uses its hollow hypostome (red) to suck blood from its host.

legs. Hard ticks also produce a sticky substance that they use to "glue" themselves to the host's skin. This substance makes the ticks very hard to remove.

Once it is in place, a tick begins to suck. It slurps blood through its hypostome like a child drinking a milkshake through a straw. The parasite's abdomen starts to bulge as blood enters the body. The abdomen may also change color. Some ticks take on a brownish-red color as they become **engorged** with blood.

A tick that is not disturbed will suck until it has eaten its fill. Depending on the tick's species and its life stage, this process can take anywhere from a few minutes to several weeks. Ticks that eat long meals may swell to dozens of times their original size before they are satisfied.

When a tick is done eating, it removes its hypostome from the host's flesh. The parasite may remain on its host while it changes into a new shape or mates. It may also drop off the host to complete these tasks.

A Long Wait

Ticks that drop off their hosts between meals sometimes have trouble catching a new ride. Why? Ticks cannot hop or fly, and they cannot crawl quickly enough to reach passing animals. They must wait until a host brushes against them. This can take a long time. Luckily, ticks' bodies are built to survive long periods without food. Some types of ticks can live for years without eating.

Ticks must be careful to avoid drying out to survive without a host. They keep their bodies moist by

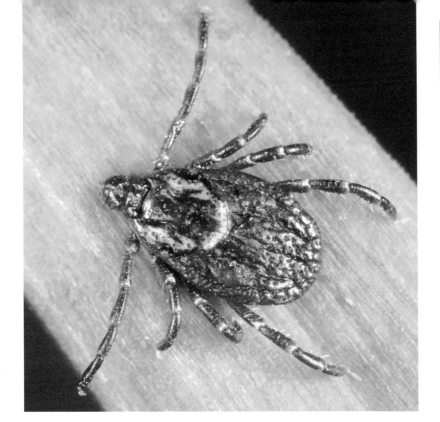

staying on the ground during the hottest parts of the day. They quest mostly in the mornings, on drizzly days, and at other times when it is damp and cool. People who know this pattern can stay out of tick-infested areas at dangerous times. By doing this they can avoid being bitten by these bloodthirsty parasites.

CHAPTER 3

Hurting the Host

In May 2000 animal-control officers in New York City were called to an apartment building to help a sick dog. When they arrived they discovered that the dog's body was seething with ticks. More than five hundred of these parasites clung to the dog, greedily drinking her blood. The dog, nearly sucked dry of blood, was so weak that she could barely move. Without help she certainly would have died.

This situation is unusual. A host does not usually carry enough ticks to drain its body of blood. People, with their mostly hairless bodies, are especially unlikely to harbor swarms of ticks. Still, even one tick can do great harm. By transmitting dangerous poisons and diseases, these parasites can sicken or even kill a human host.

A group of ticks sucks the blood from a marine toad.

Tick Paralysis

One near death occurred in Augusta, Georgia. A healthy six-year-old girl was playing happily when her fingers started to go numb. Soon she was having trouble walking. The terrified parents rushed their daughter to the local hospital. By the time they arrived, the girl could not speak clearly and she was struggling to breathe. It seemed that she might die.

But then a doctor thought to check the patient's scalp. There he found a swollen tick feasting on the girl's blood. The doctor carefully removed the tick. Immediately the girl's condition improved, and within twenty-four hours she had made a full recovery.

This girl was suffering from a condition called **tick paralysis**. Tick paralysis is caused by female ticks of certain species. When feeding, these ticks release a poison that affects the host's nerves. If the ticks are not removed, their victims can die within hours.

Disease Carriers

Although tick paralysis is scary, it is not very common. **Tick-borne** diseases, on the other hand, *are* common. About 95 percent of all **animal-borne** human infections in the United States are caused by ticks.

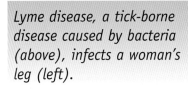

Lyme disease, a tick-borne disease caused by bacteria (above), infects a woman's leg (left).

The most common U.S. tick-borne malady is called **Lyme disease**. This illness is spread by the deer tick. Its first sign is a rash at the site of the tick's bite. The rash is in the form of a circle. If the disease is not treated right away, it spreads throughout the body. It may eventually cause arthritis, nervous system problems, heart disease, and many other problems. Victims do not usually die, but they can feel sick and weak.

One woman caught Lyme disease after cleaning a tick-infested house. Over the course of a year she experienced increasingly bad symptoms including stabbing pains, headaches, fatigue, vomiting, fever, chills, and hair loss. Her toenails fell out, her kidneys bled, and she could not sleep. Her joints ached all the time. The woman even started to lose her memory. Doctors finally cured the patient with large doses of **antibiotics**.

Other Illnesses

Ticks carry many other illnesses that affect humans. **Rocky Mountain spotted fever**, **relapsing fever**, and **encephalitis** are just a few of the tick-borne diseases that kill people every year. Forms of these diseases

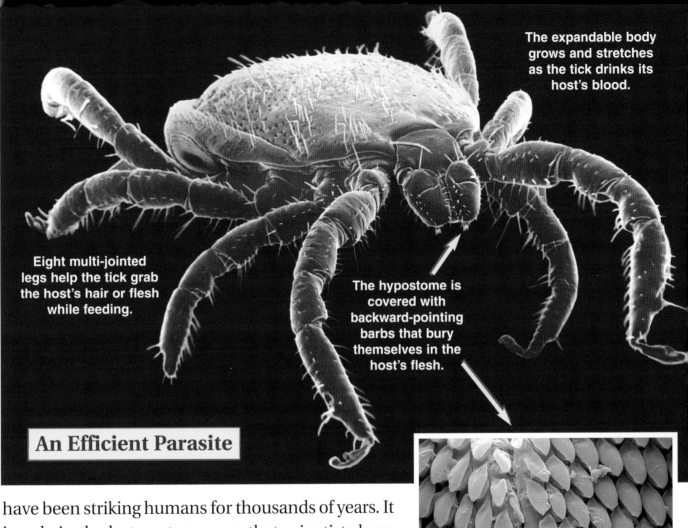

The expandable body grows and stretches as the tick drinks its host's blood.

Eight multi-jointed legs help the tick grab the host's hair or flesh while feeding.

The hypostome is covered with backward-pointing barbs that bury themselves in the host's flesh.

An Efficient Parasite

have been striking humans for thousands of years. It is only in the last century or so that scientists have had the equipment and the knowledge to track the illnesses to their source: the tick.

Controlling Ticks

Ticks are found just about everywhere in the world. These parasites are so common that it is impossible to get rid of them. Even if all the ticks in an area are killed, new ones quickly move in to take their place. But although ticks cannot be wiped out, they can be controlled.

Avoiding Ticks

Staying away from tick-infested areas is the best way to keep these tiny bloodsuckers from attacking. Grassy and wooded areas are the most dangerous places, especially when conditions are cool and damp. Avoiding these areas can reduce a person's chances of being bitten.

People who must enter tick territory can stay safe by dressing properly. Closed-toe shoes keep

Ticks are common in grassy and wooded areas.

ticks away from the feet. Long pants and long sleeves protect the legs and arms, and hats stop ticks from dropping onto the head from overhead tree branches. All clothing should be light colored to make crawling ticks easy to see and remove.

Chemicals That Kill

People can keep themselves even safer by using a pesticide called **permethrin**. Permethrin kills ticks on contact. However, it is not dangerous to humans or other animals that may be attacked by ticks. This makes permethrin safe for everyday use. This chem-

Treating pets with permethrin (right) is one way to kill bloodthirsty ticks (left).

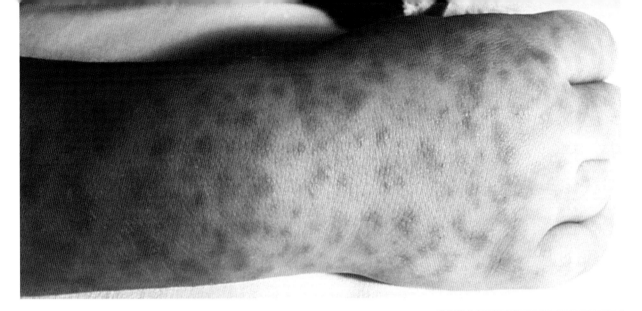

ical may be sprayed over a yard, a field, or another place where ticks live. It can even be sprayed directly onto pets' bodies, if necessary. Ticks that are touched by the deadly chemical will die.

Disease Treatment

Ticks cannot always be controlled. Sometimes they manage to bite people and make them sick. Drugs called antibiotics can usually cure tick-borne diseases—*if* they are caught early enough. Unfortunately, doing this is not always easy. Lyme disease in particular is very hard to recognize because its symptoms match so many other diseases. Sufferers may go for years without being properly treated. By the time many Lyme victims finally get the right drugs, their bodies have been permanently damaged.

Other tick-borne diseases are easier to identify. Rocky Mountain spotted fever and relapsing fever, for instance, have distinct symptoms. But these illnesses must be identified right away if treatment is to be successful. For this reason, doctors in tick-prone areas learn to recognize illnesses caused by ticks.

Preventing Disease

A few tick-borne diseases can be prevented with **vaccines**. Effective vaccines exist for Lyme disease and for Rocky Mountain spotted fever. These vaccines are not normally given. People who are at high risk for tick bites, however, can ask to be vaccinated. A vaccinated person will not become sick even if he or she is bitten by a disease-carrying tick.

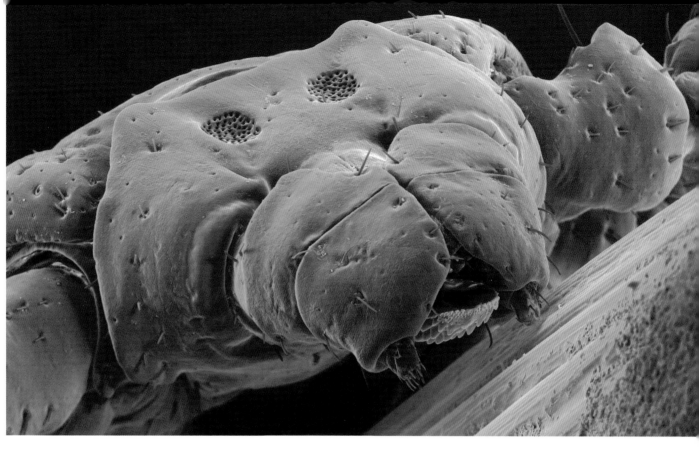

Vaccines and antibiotics are a big help in the fight against tick-borne illnesses. But it is better not to be bitten in the first place. Tick-prevention measures, therefore, are extremely important. With just a little effort, people can easily avoid becoming the victims of these bloodsucking parasites.

A brown dog tick clings to a leaf. Avoiding tick-infested areas is the best way to prevent tick-borne diseases.

abdomen: The rear body section of a tick.

animal-borne: Carried by animals.

antibiotics: Drugs that kill bacteria.

encephalitis: A viral infection spread by ticks. It causes swelling in the brain and other parts of the central nervous system.

engorged: Full of blood.

host: A plant or animal whose body provides shelter and/or food for a parasite.

hypostome: The sucking mouthpart of a tick. Pronounced "HIGH-pus-TOME."

larvae: What ticks are called right after they hatch. The first body stage in the tick's life cycle.

Lyme disease: The most widespread tick-borne illness in the United States.

nymph: The second body stage in the tick's life cycle.

parasite: A creature that lives on or feeds from another living organism.

permethrin: A pesticide that kills ticks on contact or keeps them away.

questing: A behavior pattern that some ticks use when trying to find a host.

relapsing fever: A bacterial disease spread by some soft ticks. Victims have a high fever that comes and goes many times before the illness is cured.

Rocky Mountain spotted fever: A bacterial disease caused by some hard ticks. Victims get a fever, muscle pain, headache, rash, and may die if not treated right away.

tick-borne: Carried by ticks.

tick paralysis: A disorder caused when ticks feed. The feeding ticks release a poison that paralyzes the host.

vaccine: A substance that, when taken into the body, keeps a person from getting a disease.

Books

Howard and Margery Facklam, *Parasites*. New York: Twenty-First Century Books, 1994. Read about bloodsucking parasites, invasive worms, harmful bacteria, and more in this book.

Jim Pipe, *The Giant Book of Bugs and Creepy Crawlies*. Brookfield, CT: Copper Beech, 1998. Highlights facts about insects and members of the spider family. Evolution, physical characteristics, and behavior are covered.

Alvin Silverstein, *Lyme Disease*. New York: Franklin Watts, 2001. Explains ticks and Lyme disease, with an emphasis on treatment and prevention.

Website

Dress Jessica (www.tdh.state.tx.us). Jessica is going camping with her parents. Help Jessica to pick the clothes that will protect her from tick-borne diseases.

INDEX